a NEW DAY for CRAY

Written by G Pa Rhymes &
Illustrated by Erica Leigh

Enjoy the adventures
G Pa Rhymes

Illustrations by Erica Leigh: www.EricaLeighArt.com

First paperback edition July 2020
ISBN   978-1-7348031-0-5

G Pa Rhymes Publishing
GPaRhymes.com

To my grandson Esben, my second grandchild
coming soon and all future grandbabies. May
you always have a sparkle in your eye and love
in your heart. Be kind and always play fair
even when others don't.

I miss you when you're sleeping.
Love you all the time.
When we're not together,
you're always on my mind!

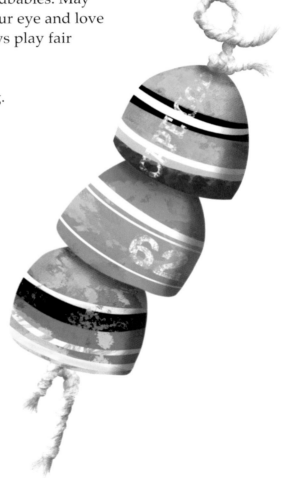

Come join me for a story
about a crab named Cray,
who loved to pinch and bully
— every single day.

He pinched and pinched not caring,
and all the creatures knew,

when Cray was somewhere near them,
he'd push right past them too.

Now, every single morning
when crawling on the beach,
he just would go on pinching
— everything in reach.

While on his daily beach crawl,
he'd stop by Turtle Fay,
to wake her and to pinch her
— every single day.

Push! Push! Push!

Pinch! Pinch! Pinch!

But today Fay saw him coming
and didn't even flinch.
She quickly swam away so
he couldn't pinch an inch.

He crawled up on the dock
to find his friend Gull Ray,
and this was his routine
— each and every day.

Pinch! Pinch! Pinch!
Tease! Tease! Tease!

But Ray did NOT enjoy it
when Cray both pinched and teased.
He really did not like it
when Cray would pinch his knees.

Now, high up on the sand dunes,
and with a watchful eye,
Fox Hay saw Cray was coming
and knew what Cray would try.

She wanted him to hear her
She had some things to say.
"Cray, NO one likes your pinching.
So, please don't play that way."

He got a little angry,
then stomped hard up and down.

Then Cray lost his balance,
and tumbled to the ground.

POP—Cray's claw flew off!
Then landed on the sand.
Cray groaned, "Oh no! Oh no… nooo!
That was my pinching hand!"

Gull Ray was flying over,
saw Cray and Hay below.
"Now, what is all the hubbub?"
Curious Ray just had to know.

An accident had happened.
Cray's life had changed that day.
Ray said, "When bad things happen,
good things will come your way."

Cray's friends had come together
to show him some support.

Now Cray seemed much less crabby;
all were happy to report.

What great news for the creatures
who wanted Cray to know,
they'd always be his friends and
they came to tell him so.

Now, Cray was feeling grateful,
so thankful for his friends.
For Cray—"This new beginning
is when the pinching ends!"

ABOUT THE AUTHOR

Break-out indie author, G Pa Rhymes (aka Gary Wakstein) has been writing raps and rhymes for more than 50 years. Until now, just for friends, family and fun. When G Pa's daughter Chelsea's son Esben was born, his son Tyler, soon to be a dad himself, said "You're a rapping, rhyming storyteller with a great imagination and a way with words. You should write some children's books to share with the world." G Pa can't keep his stories to himself any longer!

Gary lives on Cape Cod with his longtime partner and in-house editor, Liz.

"It's never too late to start something new. Just not that common at age 62!"

ABOUT THE ILLUSTRATOR

Massachusetts native Erica Leigh got her start as professional artist while pursuing her degree in Songwriting and Voice at Berklee College of Music in Boston, painting several murals on their cafeteria walls. She now works full-time balancing both careers as a musician and artist, working out of her studio with her sweet rescue dog Honey close by.

A typical day for Erica involves juggling several different projects like painting, recording, design, performance, and of course, digital illustration for fantastic authors like G Pa Rhymes!

You can find more of her work at: EricaLeighArt.com or follow her on social media @ericaleighart.

Made in the USA
Columbia, SC
30 July 2020